The Learning Works

DICTIONARY DIG

Creative Activities Designed to Get Kids Into the Dictionary

Grades 4–6

Written by Linda Schwartz • Illustrated by Beverly Armstrong

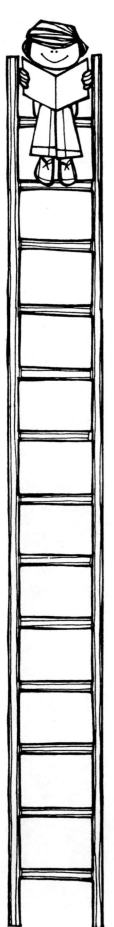

THE LEARNING WORKS

P.O. Box 6187 Santa Barbara, CA 93160

TABLE OF CONTENTS

abcdefghijklmnopqrstuvwxyz

Name _____

ALPHABETICAL SPORTS

| Words are listed in alphabetical order in the dictionary. |

Write these sports in alphabetical order as they would appear in the dictionary.

1. _____   volleyball

2. _____   golf

3. _____   ping-pong

4. _____   cricket

5. _____   basketball

6. _____   football

7. _____   soccer

8. _____   handball

9. _____   archery

10. _____   tennis

11. _____   judo

12. _____   rowing

13. _____   wrestling

14. _____   diving

15. _____   kickball

Name _____

ALPHABET MONSTERS

Write the names of these monsters in alphabetical order.

1. _____   Wolfman

2. _____   Devileye

3. _____   Beastman

4. _____   Kong King

5. _____   Spiderlegs

6. _____   Gadzilla

7. _____   Quadtooth

8. _____   Fangface

9. _____   Crazy Claws

10. _____   Tigertail

11. _____   Zooglehorn

12. _____   Jangle Jaw

Name _____

THE SECOND SCOOP

Write the ice cream flavors in alphabetical order.
(Be sure to check the second letter.)

Flavors:

Plum   Coconut
Chocolate   Boysenberry
Banana   Sarsaparilla
Strawberry   Ripple
Peach   Blueberry
Pistachio   Raspberry

Ice Cream Menu

1. _____   7. _____

2. _____   8. _____

3. _____   9. _____

4. _____   10. _____

5. _____   11. _____

6. _____   12. _____

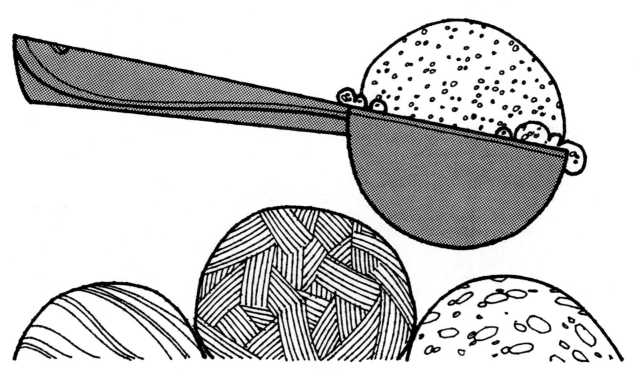

Name _____

DOGGONE DECISIONS

Write the dogs' names in each group in alphabetical order. Be sure to check the second letter.

Bowser _____   Fido _____

Benji _____   Flip _____

Blackie _____   Freddy _____

Brandy _____   Fancy _____

Bimbo _____   Fuzzy _____

Rascal _____   Duffy _____

Rover _____   Dede _____

Rufus _____   Dixie _____

Ryder _____   Dandy _____

Red _____   Doodle _____

Chippy _____   Shane _____

Cyrus _____   Sport _____

Cuddle _____   Scamp _____

Crackle _____   Snap _____

Clancy _____   Simba _____

Name _____

ALPHABET FAIR

Write each group of words in alphabetical order. Be sure to check the third letter.

capes _____   hats _____

cameras _____   hamburgers _____

candy _____   halters _____

carousel _____   hairdos _____

tents _____   ropes _____

teens _____   rolls _____

teams _____   roses _____

television _____   rockets _____

bands _____   peanuts _____

batons _____   people _____

babies _____   pegs _____

balls _____   pennants _____

laps _____   clowns _____

ladders _____   climbers _____

laughs _____   clapping _____

lamps _____   cleaning _____

Name _____

ALPHABETICAL DERBY

Help each driver find the correct car. Write each driver's name on a car in alphabetical order.

Mark   May   Manuel   Mabel   Malcolm   Mavis   Mac   Madge
Max   Maude   Matt   Mae

9

Name _____

GUIDE WORD CHECK

Guide words are listed in bold print at the top of each dictionary page. They tell the first and last words found on that page.

Look at the two guide words at the top of each page. Decide if the entry words listed would belong on that page. Write yes or no.

Example:

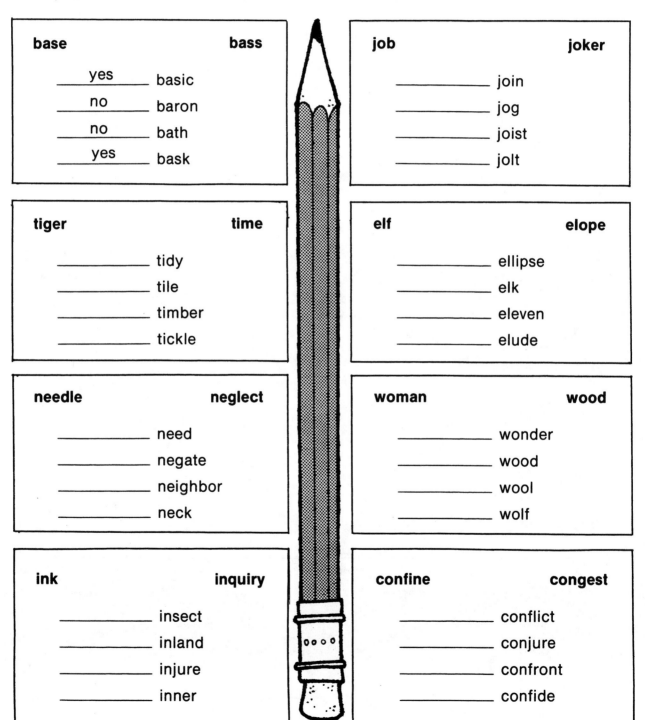

base   **bass**

____yes____ basic
____no____ baron
____no____ bath
____yes____ bask

job   **joker**

_____ join
_____ jog
_____ joist
_____ jolt

tiger   **time**

_____ tidy
_____ tile
_____ timber
_____ tickle

elf   **elope**

_____ ellipse
_____ elk
_____ eleven
_____ elude

needle   **neglect**

_____ need
_____ negate
_____ neighbor
_____ neck

woman   **wood**

_____ wonder
_____ wood
_____ wool
_____ wolf

ink   **inquiry**

_____ insect
_____ inland
_____ injure
_____ inner

confine   **congest**

_____ conflict
_____ conjure
_____ confront
_____ confide

Name _____

GUIDE WORD DETECTIVE

Guide words are given for four pages of a dictionary. Decide which words belong on each page. Write them in alphabetical order.

gang	**garlic**
_____	
_____	
_____	
_____	
_____	

gazette	**general**
_____	
_____	
_____	
_____	
_____	

gender
garden
gene
gang
gem
gap
gardenia
gargle
gelatin
gear

mat	**matrix**
_____	
_____	
_____	
_____	
_____	

matron	**may**
_____	
_____	
_____	
_____	
_____	

material
mauve
mattress
match
mature
mate
maximum
maternal
matrix
maudlin

11

Name _____

ENTRY WORD SCAVENGER HUNT

Each word defined in your dictionary is called an entry word. It is printed in bold, dark letters. An entry word can be a letter, a whole word, an abbreviation, a prefix, a suffix, a person's name, a country, or a contraction.

Use your dictionary and write an entry word for each of the following:

1. a prefix _____

2. a suffix _____

3. an abbreviation _____

4. a man _____

5. a woman _____

6. a country _____

7. a fish _____

8. a bird _____

9. a sport or game _____

10. a city _____

11. a contraction _____

12. a word starting with *k*

_____

13. a word that ends with *s*

_____

14. a word with a double consonant in the center such as *letter*

_____

✱✱✱✱✱✱✱✱ FIND FOUR ✱✱✱✱✱✱✱✱✱✱

Find four words in your dictionary that are new to you. Write the words and their definitions.

1. _____

2. _____

3. _____

4. _____

mnemonics

Name _____

PROPER PRONUNCIATION

> The dictionary shows you how to pronounce many entry words.
> The pronunciations are in parentheses. Example: **scout** (skout)

Use your dictionary and write the phonetic spelling for each word. Leave space between syllables. Show the accent marks.

1. ibis _____

2. zebu _____

3. trough _____

4. preface _____

5. bayou _____

6. reconcile _____

7. thief _____

8. intricate _____

9. rouge _____

10. unicorn _____

11. justify _____

12. warble _____

13. zephyr _____

14. chasm _____

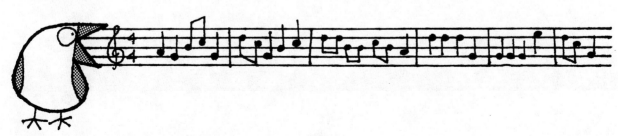

Name _____

PRONUNCIATION POWER

Look up each word in your dictionary. Write the correct pronunciation (or phonetic spelling) on the line. Underline the word that rhymes with each entry word.

Example: feign _____fān_____ sign or <u>rain</u>

1. sieve _____ receive or give

2. jib _____ crib or dive

3. crochet _____ relay or hatchet

4. pied _____ feed or hide

5. bouquet _____ forget or today

6. cache _____ mash or relay

7. queue _____ you or dewy

8. briny _____ spiny or whinny

9. quay _____ say or see

10. reign _____ pain or win

11. fife _____ knife or thief

12. filet _____ roulette or hooray

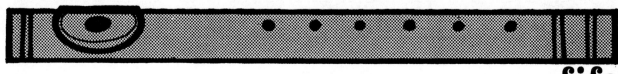

fife

Name _____

PHONETIC PICNIC

Here is a list of items you might take on a picnic. The list is written in phonetic symbols as they might be found in the dictionary. Rewrite each word, spelling it correctly. Example: sôlt <u>salt</u>

1. pep′ ər   1. _____

2. thûr′ məs   2. _____

3. bas′ kit   3. _____

4. bev′ ər ij   4. _____

5. kam′ ər ə   5. _____

6. kōl′ slô′   6. _____

7. chär′ kōl′   7. _____

8. mā ə nāz′   8. _____

9. di zûrt′   9. _____

10. tā′ bəl klôth′ 10. _____

11. sil′ vər wâr′   11. _____

12. in sek′ ti sīd′ 12. _____

13. pā′ pər plāts   13. _____

14. ham′ bûr′ gər   14. _____

15. fút′ bôl′   15. _____

Name _____

SYLLABLE SEARCH

Entry words are divided into syllables. A dictionary may use a dash, a dot, or a space to divide the word into syllables.

| Syllables help you say words correctly. | Syllables help you break a long word when you cannot fit the whole word on one line. |

bow·leg·ged bron·to·sau·rus

Go on a syllable search in your dictionary and fill in the blanks.
Divide the words into syllables.

Words with one syllable	Words with two syllables	Words with four syllables
_____	_____	_____
_____	_____	_____
_____	_____	_____
_____	_____	_____

ut·ter·ly un·com·pre·hen·si·ble

Words with five syllables
_____
_____
_____
_____

BONUS:

Super Syllable Search

Use your dictionary and see what word you can find with the most syllables. Divide your word into syllables.

_____
_____

su·per·flu·ous os·ten·ta·tious·ness

Name _____

SYLLABLE SUNDAE

Use your dictionary and divide these words into syllables. Mark the accents.

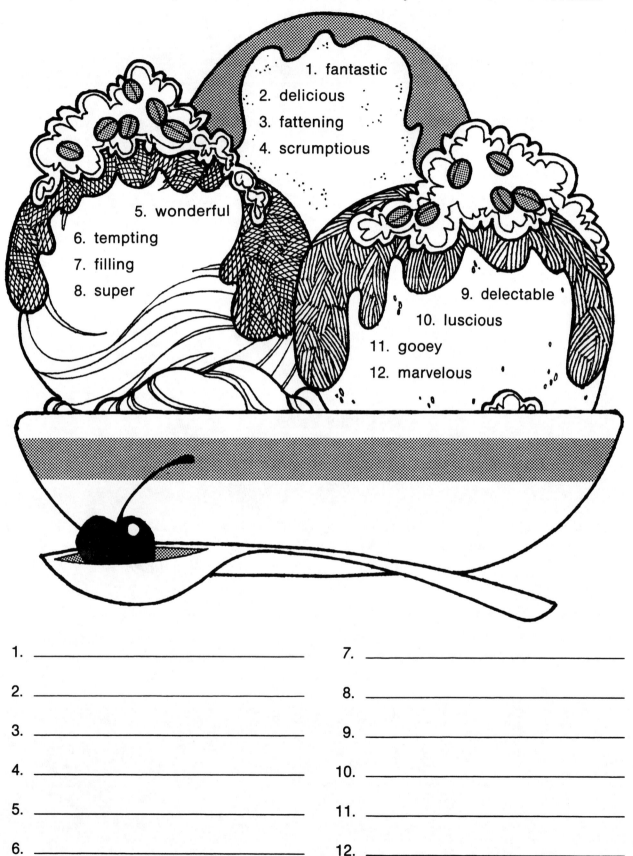

1. fantastic
2. delicious
3. fattening
4. scrumptious

5. wonderful
6. tempting
7. filling
8. super

9. delectable
10. luscious
11. gooey
12. marvelous

1. _____

2. _____

3. _____

4. _____

5. _____

6. _____

7. _____

8. _____

9. _____

10. _____

11. _____

12. _____

Name _____

MARK THE BEAT

When a word has more than one syllable, one of the syllables is said louder or with more force than the others. An accent mark (ʹ) is placed after that syllable.

Example: marʹket

Say each word below and put an accent mark (ʹ) after each accented syllable.
Check your answers with the dictionary.

1. juic—y
2. for—tune
3. dis—solve
4. ap—point
5. num—ber
6. o—pin—ion
7. im—ma—ture

8. ben—e—fit
9. in—cor—rect
10. ac—tiv—ity
11. in—cu—ba—tor
12. prin—ci—pal
13. in—di—vid—u—al
14. ad—ap—ta—tion

Tricky Trios

Look in your dictionary and find words that fit the following.
Write the words on the lines.

Three words with accents on the **second** syllable

1. _____
2. _____
3. _____

Three words with accents on the **third** syllable

1. _____
2. _____
3. _____

Three words with accents on the **fourth** syllable

1. _____
2. _____
3. _____

kan **ga** **rooʹ**

Name _____

CIRCLE A SCHWA

The schwa (ə), pronounced shwah, is a symbol used frequently in the dictionary. The schwa looks like an upside-down e. It stands for any vowel that is
spoken softly. It never sounds the same as the name of the letter.

Example: u as in b<u>u</u>n.

Circle the letter in each word that has the schwa sound. Use your dictionary for help.

1. carillon	6. margin	11. whisker
2. forbid	7. vapor	12. circus
3. agony	8. cirrus	13. purpose
4. amid	9. potato	14. zebra
5. gallivant	10. systematic	15. feature

Name _____

PICK A PART

Many dictionaries use abbreviations to show what part of speech a word is.

n. — noun (desk)	prep. — preposition (in, under)
v. — verb (jumped)	conj. — conjunction (but, or, and)
adj. — adjective (happy)	pron. — pronoun (he, she, who)
adv. — adverb (slowly)	interj. — interjection (gee! oh!)

Use your dictionary and write the part of speech for each word.

1. arum _____

2. it _____

3. nougat _____

4. snivel _____

5. gratefully _____

6. colorless _____

7. aha _____

8. juxtapose _____

9. toward _____

10. ugh _____

11. with _____

12. hapless _____

Name _____

SENTENCE SHOW-OFFS

Many words are listed as more than one part of speech in the dictionary, depending on how they are used in a sentence.

For each entry word write two sentences using the parts of speech listed.

1. **haul**

   noun _____

   verb _____

2. **mix**

   noun _____

   verb _____

3. **smooth**

   verb _____

   adj. _____

4. **under**

   prep. _____

   adv. _____

   adj. _____

5. **good**

   noun _____

   adj. _____

   interj. _____

GOOD DOG!

Name _____

PREFIX PETS

A prefix is a syllable added to the beginning of a word.
A prefix changes the meaning of the word.

Write the meaning of the prefix and give two examples of words using that prefix.

Example: <u>bi — two, twice   bicycle, bifocals</u>

	MEANING	**EXAMPLE**
1. ab—	_____	_____
2. re—	_____	_____
3. dis—	_____	_____
4. un—	_____	_____
5. pre—	_____	_____
6. mis—	_____	_____
7. ante—	_____	_____
8. tri—	_____	_____
9. co—	_____	_____
10. ex—	_____	_____

JUST FOR FUN

Draw a Prefix Pet using as many prefixes as you can.
Write the name of your Prefix Pet.

EXAMPLE

This is a bi-headed, tri-bellied, quad-footed polygurgle.

Name _____

FIX A SUFFIX

A suffix is a syllable added to the end of a word.
A suffix changes the meaning of the word.

Example: -ment means state or condition   amazement

Look up each suffix and write its meaning.
Write a word ending with each suffix.

	MEANING	EXAMPLE
1. —ic	_____	_____
2. —able	_____	_____
3. —ful	_____	_____
4. —ency	_____	_____
5. —ship	_____	_____
6. —cy	_____	_____
7. —ian	_____	_____
8. —less	_____	_____
9. —fold	_____	_____
10. —fy	_____	_____

TOOTHLESS

23

Name _____

DICTIONARY SEARCH

Some words you look up in the dictionary are not noted as entry words. You have to look up the meaning of its prefix, suffix, and/or root.

Example: unafraid — not afraid or frightened

Look at each underlined word in the sentences below.
In your own words, tell what you think the sentence means.

1. He gave me an <u>uncordial</u> welcome.

_____

2. There was a <u>disharmony</u> between the two brothers.

_____

3. We leave <u>midsummer</u> for our vacation in Canada.

_____

4. She worked as a <u>nonsalaried</u> helper for the Red Cross.

_____

5. They had to <u>repack</u> the suitcase for their trip.

_____

Name _____

HOMONYM HUNT

Homonyms are words that sound the same but are spelled differently and have different meanings.

Example: blue—blew   flour—flower

Write a sentence for each homonym listed to show that you understand the meaning of each word. Use your dictionary for help.

1. sow—sew

_____

_____

2. carrot—caret—carat

_____

_____

_____

3. cash—cache

_____

_____

4. bow—bough

_____

_____

5. reed—read

_____

_____

100

SUPER HOMONYM HUNT

Can you make a list of 100 pairs of homonyms?
Use your dictionary for help!

100

25

Name _____

SELECT A SYNONYM

Synonyms are words that are spelled and pronounced differently but have similar meanings.

Examples: <u>thin—slender</u>   <u>glad—happy</u>

Use your dictionary to help match the synonyms. Place the letter for the correct answer from Column B next to the matching synonym in Column A.

COLUMN A

- _____ 1. conducive
- _____ 2. wrangle
- _____ 3. jocund
- _____ 4. perpetual
- _____ 5. agile
- _____ 6. flashy
- _____ 7. brochure
- _____ 8. data
- _____ 9. observe
- _____ 10. marsh
- _____ 11. tedious
- _____ 12. raze
- _____ 13. summit
- _____ 14. ratify
- _____ 15. infirm

COLUMN B

- A. pamphlet
- B. tiring
- C. facts
- D. weak
- E. showy
- F. approve
- G. nimble
- H. notice
- I. helpful
- J. eternal
- K. cheerful
- L. top
- M. quarrel
- N. destroy
- O. swamp

Name _____

THE ANTONYM SAUCER

Antonyms are words that have opposite meanings.
Example: open—close

Use your dictionary and look up each word in the flying saucer.
Match each word with the correct antonym listed below.

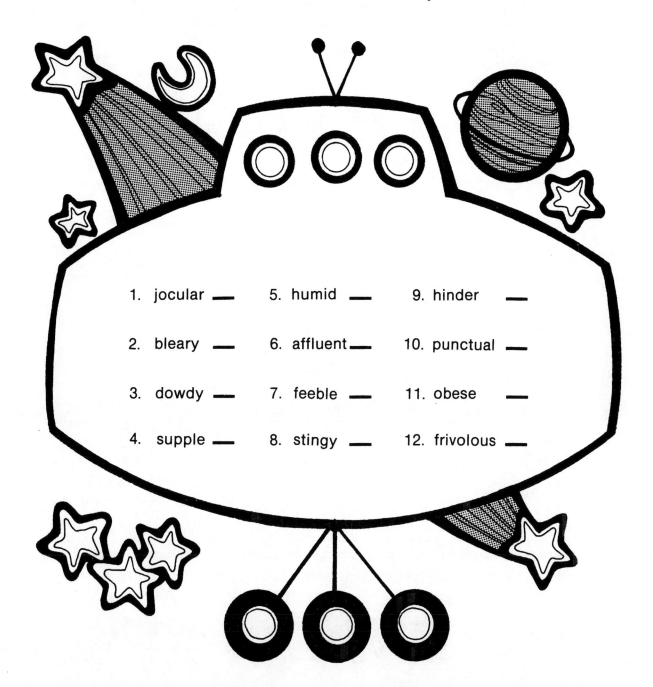

1. jocular ___
2. bleary ___
3. dowdy ___
4. supple ___

5. humid ___
6. affluent ___
7. feeble ___
8. stingy ___

9. hinder ___
10. punctual ___
11. obese ___
12. frivolous ___

A. dry
B. strong
C. sad

D. generous
E. thin
F. stylish

G. poor
H. late
I. clear

J. help
K. rigid
L. serious

Name _____

ABBREVIATED ANSWERS

Use your dictionary to see what each of these abbreviations means.
Write your answers on the lines provided.

1. inc. _____

2. yr. _____

3. FBI _____

4. EST _____

5. COD _____

6. FCC _____

7. UPI _____

8. UN _____

9. doz. _____

10. FTC _____

11. RD _____

12. etc. _____

13. misc. _____

14. AC _____

15. PTA _____

16. PST _____

one doz.

Name _____

PLURAL ROUNDUP

> The word *plural* means more than one. The dictionary gives the spelling of plural forms of many nouns. (Sometimes more than one plural spelling is listed.)
>
> Example: lasso — lassos or lassoes

Use your dictionary and write the plural of each word.

1. ox
2. abacus
3. father-in-law
4. mouse
5. ultimatum
6. genus
7. ibex

8. hero
9. intermediary
10. spoonful
11. acidity
12. junco
13. louse
14. ulna

1. _____
2. _____
3. _____
4. _____
5. _____
6. _____
7. _____

8. _____
9. _____
10. _____
11. _____
12. _____
13. _____
14. _____

Name _____

SLANG TIME

Slang words are found in the dictionary. These words are usually not accepted as proper English but are used in informal speaking.

Use your dictionary and look up each slang word.
Match each word with the correct number from the Slang Box.

_____ 1. She wore a <u>rock</u> on her finger.

_____ 2. The beggar's clothes are very <u>ratty</u>.

_____ 3. The kids <u>razzed</u> her on her birthday.

_____ 4. She is <u>nutty</u> over sausage pizza.

_____ 5. They <u>jazzed</u> up the old house with plants.

_____ 6. The spelling test was a <u>cinch</u>.

_____ 7. He had the <u>jitters</u> before the curtain went up.

_____ 8. I can <u>dig</u> what you're saying.

_____ 9. She got a <u>shiner</u> during the fight.

_____ 10. The girl acted <u>cuckoo</u> when she won the first prize.

_____ 11. The dog got into a <u>scrap</u> with the cat.

_____ 12. His grades were <u>tops</u>.

SLANG BOX

A. easy	G. understand
B. made fun of	H. diamond
C. extreme nervousness	I. crazy
D. enthusiastic	J. made lively
E. fight	K. excellent
F. black eye	L. shabby

Name _____

IDIOM CRAZE

> Idioms are combinations of words that have a special meaning. Idioms are listed in the dictionary under the most important word in the phrase. They are usually printed in small, dark type, and are found after the definition for the entry word.

Use your dictionary and write the meaning of these idioms.
Circle the entry word which you used to find the meaning.

Example: (Spring) a leak — crack and begin to let water through.

1. see eye to eye _____

2. off the record _____

3. take heart _____

4. bury the hatchet _____

5. nip and tuck _____

6. a far cry _____

7. that's that _____

8. hit it off _____

9. bring home the bacon _____

10. in full blast _____

Have fun and illustrate two idioms

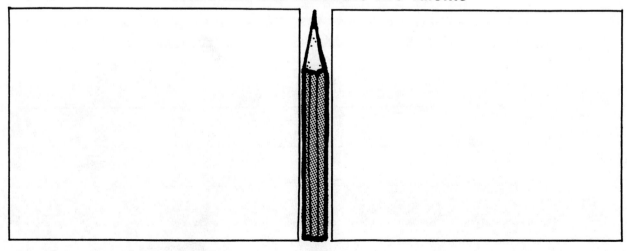

MULTIPLE MEANINGS

Some words in the dictionary are spelled and pronounced the same but have completely different meanings.

Example: firm[1] (ferm)   solid; hard

firm[2] (ferm)   a business, company or partnership

Use your dictionary and write the different meanings of these words.

1. flag   a. _____

b. _____

c. _____

2. lap   a. _____

b. _____

c. _____

3. bob   a. _____

b. _____

c. _____

4. pip   a. _____

b. _____

c. _____

5. drill   a. _____

b. _____

c. _____

✳✳✳✳✳✳✳✳✳✳✳✳✳✳✳✳✳

Name _____

PEOPLE AND PLACES

The dictionary gives information about people and places. People's names are listed last name first in alphabetical order. Use your dictionary and write the answers to the questions below.

People

1. James Edward Oglethorpe founded the colony of _____Georgia_____ .

2. Elias Howe invented the _____ .

3. Arturo Toscanini was a musical conductor from _____ .

4. What was the first name of Galileo, the famous astronomer? _____ .

5. Peter Paul Rubens was a famous _____ .

6. In Greek mythology, Medusa had _____ for hair.

7. Dwight Eisenhower, the 34th president of the U.S., was born in _____ .
   year

8. Ambrose Everett Burnside was a general in the _____ War.

Places

1. Bryce Canyon National Park is located in the state of _____ .

2. The capital of South Dakota is _____ .

3. The Galapagos Islands are found in the _____ Ocean.

4. The Ubangi refers to a _____ in Africa.

5. The Indian Ocean is _____ sq. miles.

6. Sydney is the largest city in _____ .

7. The Canary Islands are located in the _____ Ocean.

8. Yokohama is a seaport in _____

Name _____

PICTURE PUZZLES

Match the words to the pictures below.
Write the correct letter on the line by each word.
Use your dictionary for help.

_____ 1. chaps

_____ 2. octagon

_____ 3. willet

_____ 4. umbel

_____ 5. lugger

_____ 6. dingo

_____ 7. abacus

_____ 8. obelisk

_____ 9. metronome

_____ 10. zeppelin

A. B. C. D. E. F. G. H. I. J.

Name _____

DICTIONARY DRAW

Use your dictionary and find each word listed below.
Draw a picture that shows the meaning of each word.

1. Chalice

6. Akimbo

2. Isosceles

7. Oval

3. Aigrette

8. Heptagon

4. Monocle

9. Fife

5. Beret

10. Minaret

Name _____

CHOOSE A COLOR

Use your dictionary and match each color with the answers below. Write the correct letter on the line. Answers may be used more than once.

_____ 1. amber

_____ 2. carmine

_____ 3. saffron

_____ 4. dun

_____ 5. azure

_____ 6. ebony

_____ 7. indigo

_____ 8. scarlet

_____ 9. cobalt

_____ 10. emerald

_____ 11. maroon

_____ 12. cerulean

_____ 13. umber

_____ 14. ultramarine

_____ 15. crimson

_____ 16. chartreuse

yellow	red	blue	black	green	brown
A	B	C	D	E	F

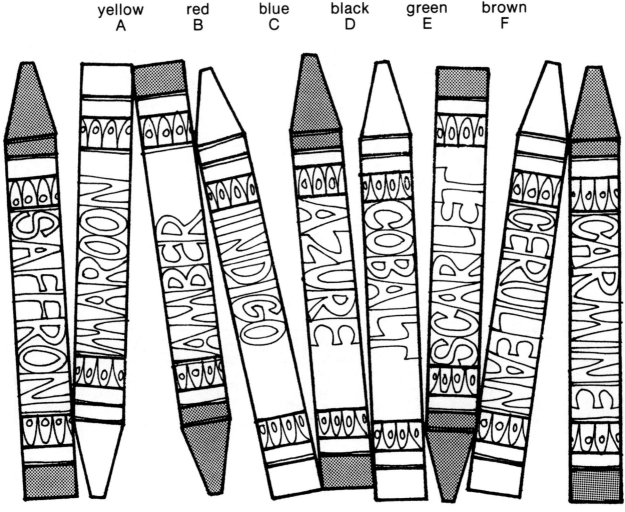

Name _____

PICK A PLANT

In the garden below are the names of six flowers or plants.
Use your dictionary and list the six.

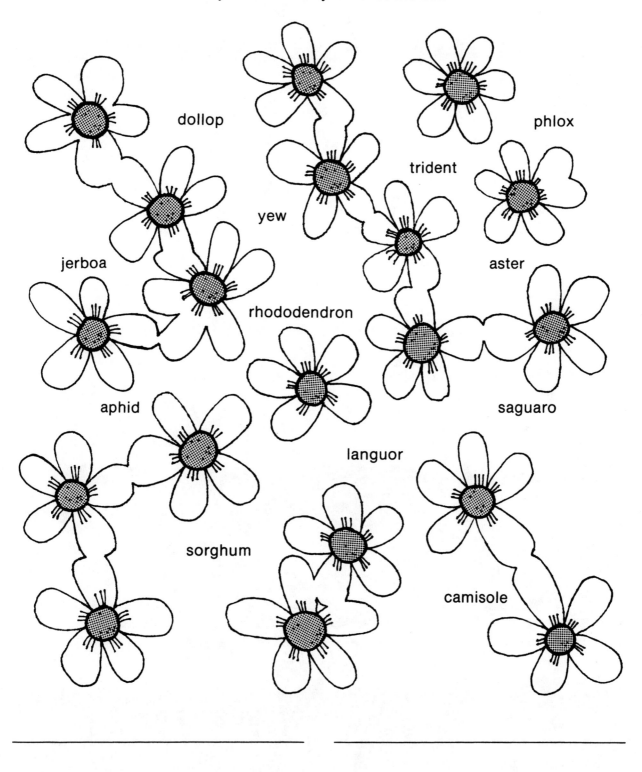

dollop

phlox

trident

yew

jerboa

rhododendron

aster

aphid

saguaro

languor

sorghum

camisole

_____   _____

_____   _____

_____   _____

Name _____

WHO'S WHO?

Listed below are the names of mammals and birds.
Look up each word in your dictionary. Write (M) mammal or (B) bird for each word.

_____ 1. snipe

_____ 2. vole

_____ 3. kiwi

_____ 4. rhea

_____ 5. quetzal

_____ 6. gnu

_____ 7. eland

_____ 8. jackdaw

_____ 9. rook

_____ 10. addax

_____ 11. plover

_____ 12. osprey

_____ 13. wombat

_____ 14. yak

_____ 15. koala

_____ 16. wolverine

_____ 17. ibis

_____ 18. puffin

_____ 19. shrew

_____ 20. dobbin

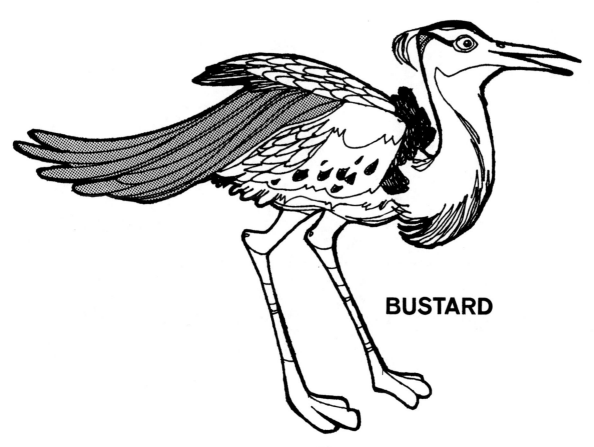

BUSTARD

Name _____

MENU MEANINGS

Use your dictionary to see what each word on the menu means. Match the definitions by placing the correct letter in front of each word on the menu.

MENU

_____ 1. abalone

_____ 2. pomegranate

_____ 3. eclair

_____ 4. jujube

_____ 5. succotash

_____ 6. kale

_____ 7. pimiento

_____ 8. caviar

_____ 9. leek

_____ 10. anchovy

_____ 11. brisket

_____ 12. chicory

_____ 13. filbert

_____ 14. romaine

_____ 15. ricotta

_____ 16. chard

_____ 17. molasses

_____ 18. quail

_____ 19. cider

_____ 20. compote

A. fish	F. sweet pepper	K. lettuce	P. mollusk
B. candy	G. herbs	L. onion	Q. bird
C. beet	H. juice	M. stewed fruit	R. cabbage
D. meat	I. corn and beans	N. nut	S. cheese
E. fruit	J. syrup	O. pastry	T. fish eggs

Name _____

AROUND THE WORLD

For each word, match the luggage tag representing the place where each can be found. Use your dictionary for help.

_____ 1. kiwi

_____ 2. sari

_____ 3. bola

_____ 4. poi

_____ 5. budgerigar

_____ 6. balboa

_____ 7. fjord

_____ 8. umiak

_____ 9. samovar

_____ 10. jinrikisha

_____ 11. okapi

_____ 12. rathskeller

_____ 13. frijol

_____ 14. bairn

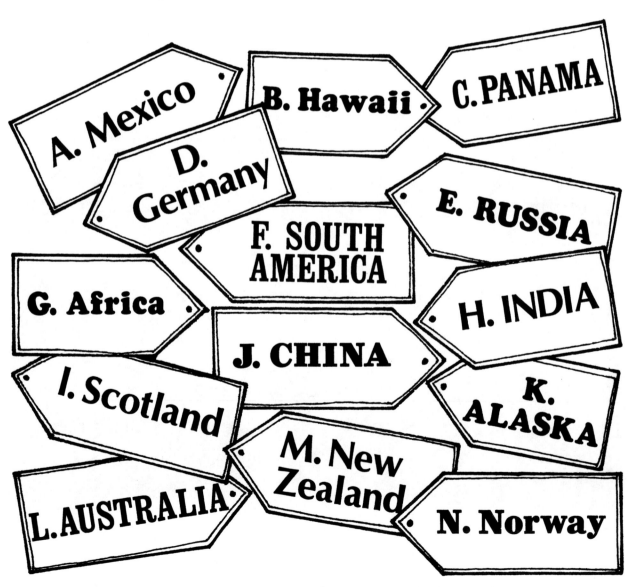

Name _____

WHAT WOULD YOU DO WITH?

Use your dictionary and circle the <u>best</u> answer.

1. What would you do with a hyacinth?
   a. eat it
   b. sing it
   c. wear it
   d. plant it

2. What would you do with an epaulet?
   a. bury it
   b. chain it
   c. wear it
   d. play it

3. What would you do with a landau?
   a. ride in it
   b. staple it
   c. row it
   d. fry it

4. What would you do with a piccolo?
   a. hide it
   b. play it
   c. tie it down
   d. cook it

5. What would you do with a prawn?
   a. play chess with it
   b. eat it
   c. bat it
   d. wear it

6. What would you do with a hexagon?
   a. broil it
   b. cage it
   c. measure it
   d. exercise it

7. What would you do with a snood?
   a. wear it
   b. paint it
   c. bake it
   d. chop it up

8. What would you do with a howdah?
   a. fly in it
   b. swim in it
   c. ride in it
   d. sail in it

Name _____

WHERE WOULD YOU FIND?

Use your dictionary and circle the <u>best</u> answer.

1. Where would you find a clavicle?
   a. in an orchestra
   b. on the beach
   c. in your body
   d. on a car

2. Where would you find a joist?
   a. on the ceiling
   b. in a tournament
   c. in the ocean
   d. in your arm

3. Where would you find a millipede?
   a. in the freezer
   b. on the ground
   c. on the grocery shelf
   d. in a shoe store

4. Where would you find a gemsbok?
   a. in a jewelry store
   b. in a bathtub
   c. in the zoo
   d. in a hotel

5. Where would you find a zwieback?
   a. in the grocery store
   b. in the zoo
   c. in the swimming pool
   d. in a rock band

6. Where would you find a stalagmite?
   a. in a clothing store
   b. in a barber shop
   c. on the beach
   d. in a cave

7. Where would you find the Eiffel Tower?
   a. in London
   b. in Paris
   c. in Switzerland
   d. in the U.S.

8. Where would you find an incisor?
   a. in your mouth
   b. in the oven
   c. in a pet shop
   d. on a scissor

Name _____

LABEL THE LICENSES

Use your dictionary to help match each occupation with the personalized license plates that tell the thing each person would be most likely to study.

CLUE BOX

A. ichthyologist   E. zoologist   I. podiatrist

B. anthropologist   F. botanist   J. pharmacist

C. economist   G. audiologist   K. entomologist

D. agronomist   H. hydrologist   L. etymologist

1. | SOIL | 2. | WATER | 3. | PLANTS |

4. | ANIMALS | 5. | INSECTS | 6. | FISH |

7. | WORDS | 8. | MONEY | 9. | DRUGS |

10. | MAN | 11. | FEET | 12. | EARS |

Use your dictionary and draw license plates for an optometrist and a chemist.

CREATE YOUR OWN DICTIONARY

1. Make up a word you have never heard before.

2. Look up your word in the dictionary. If you find it there, make up a new word. Your word must be original.

3. Write your new word in large letters across the top of a piece of white art paper.

4. Write the correct part of speech for your word.
    (Is your word a noun, verb, adjective, adverb?)

5. Divide your word into syllables and mark the accent or stress mark so other students will know how to pronounce your word.

6. Draw a picture of your word to show others what it means.

7. Write a definition or tell what your word means in one or two sentences.

8. Use your word in a sentence.

MISHYMUSHILY (Adv.)
Mish—y—mush´—i—ly

This means in a squishy sort of way.

The moose moved mishymushily across the muddy marsh.

Answers

Page 4

1. archery
2. basketball
3. cricket
4. diving
5. football
6. golf
7. handball
8. judo
9. kickball
10. ping-pong
11. rowing
12. soccer
13. tennis
14. volleyball
15. wrestling

Page 5

1. Beastman
2. Crazy Claws
3. Devileye
4. Fangface
5. Gadzilla
6. Jangle Jaw
7. Kong King
8. Quadtooth
9. Spiderlegs
10. Tigertail
11. Wolfman
12. Zooglehorn

Page 6

1. Banana
2. Blueberry
3. Boysenberry
4. Chocolate
5. Coconut
6. Peach
7. Pistachio
8. Plum
9. Raspberry
10. Ripple
11. Sarsaparilla
12. Strawberry

Page 7

Benji
Bimbo
Blackie
Bowser
Brandy

Fancy
Fido
Flip
Freddy
Fuzzy

Rascal
Red
Rover
Rufus
Ryder

Dandy
Dede
Dixie
Doodle
Duffy

Chippy
Clancy
Crackle
Cuddle
Cyrus

Scamp
Shane
Simba
Snap
Sport

Page 8

cameras
candy
capes
carousel

hairdos
halters
hamburgers
hats

teams
teens
television
tents

rockets
rolls
ropes
roses

Page 8 — continued

babies
balls
bands
batons

peanuts
pegs
pennants
people

ladders
lamps
laps
laughs

clapping
cleaning
climbers
clowns

Page 9

1. Mabel
2. Mac
3. Madge
4. Mae
5. Malcolm
6. Manuel
7. Mark
8. Matt
9. Maude
10. Mavis
11. Max
12. May

Page 10

job—joker
yes
yes
yes
no

tiger—time
no
yes
yes
no

elf—elope
yes
yes
no
no

needle—neglect
no
yes
no
no

woman—wood
yes
yes
no
no

ink—inquiry
no
yes
no
yes

confine—congest
yes
no
yes
no

Page 11

gang—garlic
gang
gap
garden
gardenia
gargle

mat—matrix
match
mate
material
maternal
matrix

gazette—general
gear
gelatin
gem
gender
gene

matron—may
mattress
mature
maudlin
mauve
maximum

TIGERTAIL

Page 12

Answers will vary.

Page 13

1. ī′ bis
2. zē′ bū
3. trôf
4. pref′ is
5. bī′ ü
6. rek′ ən sil
7. thēf
8. in′ trə kit
9. rüzh
10. ū′ nə kôrn
11. jus′ tə fī
12. wôr′ bəl
13. zef′ ər
14. kaz′ əm

Page 14

1. siv — give
2. jib — crib
3. krō shā′ — relay
4. pīd — hide
5. bō kā′ or bu ka′ — today
6. kash — mash
7. kū — you
8. brin′ i — spiny
9. kē — see
10. rān — pain
11. fīf — knife
12. fi-lā′ — hooray

Page 15

1. pepper
2. Thermos
3. basket
4. beverage
5. camera
6. cole slaw
7. charcoal
8. mayonnaise
9. dessert
10. tablecloth
11. silverware
12. insecticide
13. paper plates
14. hamburger
15. football

Page 16

Answers will vary.

Page 17

1. fan-tas′-tic
2. de-li′-cious
3. fat′-ten-ing
4. scrump′-tious
5. won′-der-ful
6. tempt′-ing
7. fill′-ing
8. su′-per
9. de-lec′-ta-ble
10. lus′-cious
11. goo′-ey
12. mar′-vel-ous

Page 18

1. juic′-y
2. for′-tune
3. dis-solve′
4. ap-point′
5. num′-ber
6. o-pin′-ion
7. im-ma-ture′
8. ben′-e-fit
9. in-cor-rect′
10. ac-tiv′-i-ty
11. in′-cu-ba-tor
12. prin′-ci-pal
13. in-di-vid′-u-al
14. ad-ap-ta′-tion

Page 19

1. i
2. o
3. o
4. a
5. i
6. i
7. o
8. u
9. o
10. e
11. e
12. u
13. o
14. a
15. u

Page 20

1. n.
2. pron.
3. n.
4. v.
5. adv.
6. adj.
7. interj.
8. v.
9. prep.
10. interj.
11. prep.
12. adj.

Page 21

Answers will vary.

pron.

Page 22 — Examples will vary.

1. from, away, away from
2. again, anew, once more
3. opposite of
4. not
5. before in time, order, or place
6. bad, wrong
7. before
8. three having three parts
9. with, together, joint, equally
10. out of, from

Page 23 — Examples will vary.

1. of or having to do with
2. capable of
3. full of
4. state of being
5. office or rank
6. position, office
7. the same as
8. without, that does not
9. times as many
10. make, cause to be

Page 24

Answers will vary.

Page 25

Answers will vary.

Page 26

1. I
2. M
3. K
4. J
5. G
6. E
7. A
8. C
9. H
10. O
11. B
12. N
13. L
14. F
15. D

Page 27

1. C	7. B
2. I	8. D
3. F	9. J
4. K	10. H
5. A	11. E
6. G	12. L

Page 28

1. incorporated
2. year
3. Federal Bureau of Investigation
4. Eastern Standard Time
5. Cash on delivery or
   Collect on delivery
6. Federal Communications Commission
7. United Press International
8. United Nations
9. dozen
10. Federal Trade Commission
11. rural delivery
12. et cetera
13. miscellaneous
14. alternating current
15. Parent-Teacher Association
16. Pacific Standard Time

Page 29

1. oxen	8. heroes
2. abacuses or abaci	9. intermediaries
3. fathers-in-law	10. spoonfuls, spoonsful
4. mice	11. acidities
5. ultimatums, ultimata	12. juncos, juncoes
6. genera, genuses	13. lice
7. ibexes, ibices	14. ulnas, ulnae

Page 30

1. H	5. J	9. F
2. L	6. A	10. I
3. B	7. C	11. E
4. D	8. G	12. K

Page 31 — Answers may vary slightly.

1. eye — agree entirely
2. record — not to be recorded
3. heart — be encouraged
4. hatchet — make peace
5. nip — even in a race or contest
6. cry — a long way; a great difference
7. that — that is settled or decided
8. hit — get along well together; agree
9. bacon — be successful; win the prize
10. blast — in full operation

Page 32 — Answers may vary.

1. a. piece of cloth with a pattern
   b. Iris
   c. get tired
2. a. front part of a body from waist to knees
      when sitting down
   b. lapping over
   c. drink by lifting with tongue
3. a. move up and down with short motions
   b. short haircut
   c. seize with teeth
4. a. seed
   b. disease of birds
   c. spot on dice or dominoes
   d. peep; chirp
5. a. tool for boring holes
   b. machine for planting seeds
   c. strong cloth
   d. baboon of Africa

Page 33

1. Georgia	1. Utah
2. sewing machine	2. Pierre
3. Italy	3. Pacific
4. Galilei	4. river
5. painter	5. 28,350,000
6. snakes	6. Australia
7. 1890	7. Atlantic
8. Civil	8. Japan

Page 34

1. E	6. F
2. J	7. A
3. B	8. I
4. H	9. G
5. D	10. C

Page 35

Answers will vary.

Page 36

1. A	5. C	9. C	13. F
2. B	6. D	10. E	14. C
3. A	7. C	11. B	15. B
4. F	8. B	12. C	16. E

Page 37 — in any order.

1. phlox
2. yew
3. rhododendron
4. sorghum
5. saguaro
6. aster

Page 38

1. B	6. M	11. B	16. M
2. M	7. M	12. B	17. B
3. B	8. B	13. M	18. B
4. B	9. B	14. M	19. M
5. B	10. M	15. M	20. M

Page 39

1. P
2. E
3. O
4. B
5. I
6. R
7. F
8. T
9. L
10. A
11. D
12. G
13. N
14. K
15. S
16. C
17. J
18. Q
19. H
20. M

Page 40

1. M
2. H
3. F
4. B
5. L
6. C
7. N
8. K
9. E
10. J
11. G
12. D
13. A
14. I

Page 41

1. d
2. c
3. a
4. b
5. b
6. c
7. a
8. c

Page 42

1. c
2. a
3. b
4. c
5. a
6. d
7. b
8. a

Page 43

1. D
2. H
3. F
4. E
5. K
6. A
7. L
8. C
9. J
10. B
11. I
12. G